Hope

by Barbara A. Donovan
illustrated by Joan Waites

Harcourt
SCHOOL PUBLISHERS

Printed in China

ISBN 10: 0-15-350302-5
ISBN 13: 978-0-15-350302-3

Ordering Options
ISBN 10: 0-15-349941-9 (Grade 6 ELL Collection)
ISBN 13: 978-0-15-349941-8 (Grade 6 ELL Collection)
ISBN 10: 0-15-357342-2 (package of 5)
ISBN 13: 978-0-15-357342-2 (package of 5)

5 6 7 8 9 10   0940   12 11 10 09

It is 1933. The United States is in the middle of the Great Depression. People have no money because there is very little work. For farmers in Oklahoma, the trouble is not just the lack of money. The trouble is the lack of rain, too. Their land used to be green with crops. Now it is dust. In fact, their land has a new name: the Dust Bowl.

I'm afraid. I'm afraid of so many things right now. I'm afraid that we will lose our farm. I'm afraid that I'll never see Papa again. He has gone to work for Uncle Ned in the city. I'm afraid that Ma will never smile again. I'm afraid that I will never have the chance to reach my dreams.

I want so much to be a writer someday. I have always had stories in my head. I used to write my stories in a black notebook. However, I've already filled each page. There isn't space for another word. We can't afford another notebook. Instead, I keep all my new stories in my memory. I hope to have money to buy another notebook someday.

Right now I'm on my way to school. Normally, I'd be excused from school at this time of year to help with the harvest. This year we have no harvest. The wheat we planted dried up in the summer heat. The stream I used to play in is as dusty as the road on which I'm walking.

Our schoolhouse used to be white. It is now brown. The dust blows everywhere. I look around the room as I enter. I take my seat. Miss Harper is writing our exercises for the day on the chalkboard. The Wilson boys, Len and Glen, are whispering. My friend Ginny smiles shyly at me. The four of us are the only students left. Everyone else moved away so their families could look for work on the farms out west.

I'm scared that our school might be closed. School is the only place where I can write. Miss Harper begged for paper from some companies in town. The paper has writing on one side. Still, I don't mind.

Miss Harper always begins our school day with the newspaper. She buys the newspaper each day. The newspaper is her only luxury. None of our families can afford a newspaper even though it is only a few pennies. Each day, we take turns reading the stories on the front page.

Today Miss Harper asks us to turn to page eight. We look at the articles. We do not notice anything special. Then Miss Harper points out a small article. I wouldn't have seen it if she had not told us. It says that the newspaper is having a writing contest. The top prize is fifty dollars. That's a fortune!

We ask questions all at once. Before long, Miss Harper settles us down. Miss Harper says we will need to write a story about the happiest time in our life.

When I go home, I tell Ma about the contest over supper. Then I tell her I don't have much of a chance of winning. Ma says to me, "Frannie, you are the best writer I've ever known. Do your best. Then go back and make it better. Trust yourself."

I have some hope for the first time in a long time. Maybe I can win this contest if I really try. I have a hard time sleeping. Ideas for my story spin in my brain as I toss and turn.

When Ma wakes me for school in the morning,
I know exactly what to write about. Sleeping and
resting my brain helped. I can't wait for school
to start. I race to school as fast as I can. I'm even
a bit impatient as we read the newspaper. Finally,
Miss Harper takes one sheet of her precious supply
of paper. She cuts it into quarters. She gives each
of us one piece. Then she tells us to quickly write
down our topic. When was the happiest time in
our life and why?

I'm smiling as I write because my ideas bring back happy memories. I write very tiny letters so that I can fit a lot on my little square of paper. Soon Miss Harper tells us time is up. She collects our papers. She reads them as we work on our math assignments.

Once in a while, I look at Miss Harper as she reads. Sometimes she looks puzzled. Sometimes she looks pleased. I can't tell whose paper gets which reaction. Miss Harper writes her comments in red pencil on the back of each paper. She hands the papers back to us.

My heart is thumping. I turn my paper over so that I can read her comments on the back. I can't stop smiling. Miss Harper writes, "What will you do with the fifty dollars when you win, Frannie?"

For the next week in school, we work on our stories. We write drafts. We read them to each other. Little by little, my story improves. Then Miss Harper gives us each a clean, unused sheet of paper for our final stories. I'm a bit afraid to put my pencil on the paper. What if my story isn't good enough? Then I remember Ma's words: "Trust yourself." I start to write. Before long, Miss Harper collects our papers. She puts them in a large envelope. She'll deliver them to the newspaper office after school.

For weeks, I look through the paper for news about the contest. One day, Miss Harper introduces a surprise guest to the class. Mr. Graves is the editor of the newspaper. He says, "Thank you for all of your wonderful stories. One story from your class grabbed my attention. It's the story of a girl whose happiest times were the simple times with her family. She wrote about the times when she'd work beside her mother making blueberry pies. She wrote about her father reading aloud *Treasure Island* as she fell asleep each night."

My classmates begin staring at me with each word that Mr. Graves speaks. They know, just as I do, that this is my story. I'm thrilled and scared at the same time. Does this mean I've won the writing contest?

Then Mr. Graves says, "I wanted to come to congratulate the writer of this story. She has won second prize in the contest."

I've won second prize! He calls me to the front of the room. He hands me a large envelope. Inside is a crisp new ten-dollar bill. I'm not rich. However, ten dollars sure makes me feel rich. Better than the money is what else is in the envelope—a brand new notebook! Now I can write all those stories that fill my head. I can't wait to run home and tell Ma. I know she will be proud.

Scaffolded Language Development

USING COMPOUND DEVELOPMENT Write the following words from the story on the board: *notebook, schoolhouse, newspaper, chalkboard,* and *blueberry*. Explain that these words are compound words. They are made up of two shorter words that have been put together. Draw a line between the two words in each compound word. Then have students chorally say each compound word as the two words that make it up.

Have students say the words in each column and then match each word in column 1 to a word in column 2 to make a compound word:

Column 1	Column 2
base	light
back	ball
flash	pack
finger	nail

Ask students to write each word and discuss its meaning.

Language Arts

Compound Formula Using the equation *base + ball = baseball*, have students create their own compound word flashcards. Ask students to write and draw a picture of the compound word on the back of each card. Then encourage them to practice compound words with the cards they made.

School-Home Connection

School Days Have students discuss with family members important things the family members learned in school or that their parents taught them.

Word Count: 1,165